ADVANCE PRAISE FOR

Seeing Red

We teach kids important skills like reading and writing so they can get along
in the world. We also need to teach kids the key skills needed
to get along with other people. Anger management is one of those
crucial skills and *Seeing Red* is a wonderful step by step program
to teach children how to do it.
-- DAVID WALSH, PH.D., PRESIDENT, NATIONAL INSTITUTE
ON MEDIA AND THE FAMILY

The *Seeing Red* curriculum has been helpful for my students, enabling
them to think about specific situations, to break them down, and
to recreate new ways of handling their anger. Students have
an opportunity to learn that everyone gets angry and that it is
a normal feeling. This curriculum helps them understand
different and more positive ways of expressing their anger.
– LESLIE COLERIN, SCHOOL SOCIAL WORKER,
ANNE SULLIVAN COMMUNICATION CENTER

The *Seeing Red* curriculum is very well laid out for the facilitator.
It offers interactive activities to bring about discussion on
a very serious topic, and does so in a fun and effective manner.
Each lesson builds upon the others, creating a comprehensive
and thorough curriculum that fosters learning and an understanding
of anger as an emotion, and that it is how we deal with anger
that makes a difference.
– JULIE NEITZEL CARR, RESOLUTION AND PREVENTION PROGRAM,
YWCA OF MINNEAPOLIS

Seeing Red

an anger management and peacemaking curriculum for kids

Seeing Red

an anger management
and peacemaking curriculum
for kids

A RESOURCE FOR TEACHERS, SOCIAL WORKERS,
AND YOUTH LEADERS

Jennifer Simmonds
Family & Children's Service

NEW SOCIETY PUBLISHERS

Cataloguing in Publication Data:
A catalog record for this publication is available from the National Library of Canada.

Cover design by Diane McIntosh, illustration by Lydia English.

Printed in Canada by Friesens.

New Society Publishers acknowledges the support of the Government of Canada through the Book Publishing Industry Development Program (BPIDP) for our publishing activities.

Paperback ISBN: 0-86571-483-5

Inquiries regarding requests to reprint all or part of *Seeing Red* should be addressed to New Society Publishers at the address below.

To order directly from the publishers, please add $4.50 shipping to the price of the first copy, and $1.00 for each additional copy (plus GST in Canada). Send check or money order to:

New Society Publishers
P.O. Box 189, Gabriola Island, BC V0R 1X0, Canada
1-800-567-6772

New Society Publishers' mission is to publish books that contribute in fundamental ways to building an ecologically sustainable and just society, and to do so with the least possible impact on the environment, in a manner that models this vision. We are committed to doing this not just through education, but through action. We are acting on our commitment to the world's remaining ancient forests by phasing out our paper supply from ancient forests worldwide. This book is one step towards ending global deforestation and climate change. It is printed on acid-free paper that is 100% old growth forest-free (100% post-consumer recycled), processed chlorine free, and printed with vegetable based, low VOC inks. For further information, or to browse our full list of books and purchase securely, visit our website at: www.newsociety.com

NEW SOCIETY PUBLISHERS
www.newsociety.com

Dedication

Seeing Red is dedicated to the thousands of Minnesota children who have participated in *Keep the Peace* groups, facilitated by Family & Children's Service. These young people, who struggle with their anger daily, have prevailed as peacemakers and positive leaders. We applaud them for their courage and determination, and we commend the hundreds of teachers, social workers and youth leaders who work with them to create safe, peaceful and nurturing learning environments.

Table of Contents

Introduction

Program Objectives

Everyone feels angry at times. By itself, anger is not a problem. It is simply a feeling, just like feeling happy, excited, scared or sad. However, if it's being stuffed or becomes explosive, anger can turn harmful and destructive. Eventually, our anger can control everything we do and damage important relationships with others.

Seeing Red is a curriculum designed to help elementary and middle-school aged students better understand their anger so they can make healthy and successful choices and build strong relationships. The overall objectives of *Seeing Red* are for participants to realize that they can control their behavior and develop practical skills and strategies to manage their feelings, which in turn will increase their self-esteem. The objectives of the curriculum are achieved through role playing common situations, identifying associated feelings, doing problem solving, recognizing negative behaviors, and anticipating consequences.

Design and Framework of Lesson Plans

This 12-week curriculum is specifically designed for a small group (six to eight participants) of elementary or middle-school-aged children who are willing to participate in such a group. The ideal group should convene weekly in a confidential space with the same group members and facilitators attending each session. The curriculum is meant to be used in consecutive order because, as the lessons progress, group members will build upon skills learned from previous lessons. However, some of the middle sessions can be eliminated, combined, or moved around to customize specific needs and goals of the group.

Each session includes objectives for that particular lesson, a list of supplies needed for the various activities, a description of tasks to be done prior to the start of the lesson, background notes to the leader, a warm-up activity at the start of each meeting, an explanation of the various learning activities, and a closing activity.

Important Note

The ★ symbol located in various lesson plans indicates that a particular activity would be best suited for middle school-aged or older participants, and should be substituted for the other described activity for groups with young participants.

Key Concepts of *Seeing Red*

- Identify common triggers of anger.
- Take responsibility for mistakes.
- Identify positive and healthy ways to keep from losing control.
- Explore how participants cover up more painful feelings with anger.
- Discern how people provoke participants (and vice versa) as a means of control.
- Empower group members as peacemakers.
- Recognize how family members express anger and how that can influence how participants express their anger.
- Better understand the motivation and harm behind bullying.

Key Activities of *Seeing Red*

- Establish trust within the group.
- Practice stating feelings, and the positive results being sought from the other person.
- Develop positive and realistic problem-solving skills.
- Learn and practice five key steps to controlling anger.
- Generate ideas for creating peace in our world.
- Explore the natural consequences of choices.
- Practice diffusing situations through what is said and how it's said.

Facilitating Effective Groups

A unique aspect of the *Seeing Red* curriculum is its specific design for small groups of willing participants. As a result, group members are more willing to learn from one another and empower each other. This group process helps participants build upon other important developmental skills as well. For example, leadership skills (taking initiative, presenting in front of the group, offering ideas), social skills (taking turns, cooperating, active listening), and building self-esteem (positive feedback from peers, problem solving, empowering the group) are all components of small group work that are integrated into the *Seeing Red* curriculum.

As is true with most curricula, lessons plans can be modified or changed in order to best meet the needs of a particular group. However, following is a list of overall helpful hints that can greatly increase the success of a group:

➢ **Group Compositon Is Crucial!** Be thoughtful about whom you invite as a part of the group. There should be a mixture of personalities and behaviors in the group (for example, only participants who have a history of repeated behavior problems would not likely be a productive group). Also, participants should be no more than one or two years apart in age or grade.

➢ **Keep The Group Small.** The ideal group size for *Seeing Red* is between five and seven participants.

➢ **Keep The Same Participants.** In order to build trust and group cohesion, it's important to maintain the same participants throughout all the sessions. If a group member leaves the group midway through, it's not recommended to fill his or her space with a new group member.

➢ **Consistency.** Each session is designed to build upon the previous lesson's skills. Therefore, it's important to meet consistently (recommended once a week), in the same space with the same group members and adult facilitator(s).

➢ **Use Teachable Moments.** If a conflict arises among participants during a session, address it immediately (but be careful not to shame those involved in the conflict). Use the "real life" scenario as a teachable moment and ask other group members to assist in problem solving.

➢ **Accountability.** As a group facilitator, hold the participants accountable for the rules that they create during the first session. Also, be sure to affirm their positive behavior and thoughtful ideas.

WELCOME WEEK
SESSION ONE

LESSON OBJECTIVES

⇒ Establish trust in the group.

⇒ Create group rules and guidelines.

⇒ Identify different triggers of anger.

⇒ Identify different reactions to anger.

SUPPLIES NEEDED

☑ Blank 8 ½" x 11" paper for each group member, folded in thirds

☑ Flipchart pad or other large sheets of paper

☑ Markers, pencils/pens

☑ Copies of "When I get mad I…" worksheet

☑ Folder for each participant (optional)

BEFORE THE MEETING

Read through the lesson and collect necessary supplies. Make sure that the activities you've chosen are age-appropriate for your group. Secure a quiet, confidential space for the group to meet.

NOTES TO THE LEADER

This is the first group session in a sequence of 12 meetings. The primary purpose of this lesson is to build group cohesion and lay the groundwork for future meetings.

Often, participants assume they're in a group like this because of their frequent poor behavior. Regardless of whether that's true, it's up to the faciliator to reassure group members that the purpose isn't to focus on negative behavior, but to find healthy and helpful ways of dealing with their anger. Everyone can use this help.

A.   NAME-TENT INTRODUCTIONS

 20 min.

Distribute to each person a blank, 8 ½" x 11" piece of paper, folded length-wise in thirds, to form a "name-tent." Ask group members use the markers to write and decorate their first names on the front of their tents.

Also on their name-tents, they should draw two pictures of something about themselves to share with the group.

Go around the circle and have each person talk about the drawings on his/her name-tent. Stand the name-tents up on the table so everyone can see. (Collect the name-tents after the session to use for the following sessions.)

B.   ONE TRUTH, ONE LIE

Each group member, one at a time, tells two things about him/herself, one that is true and one that is false. (Example: "I have three sisters," and "I don't like hamburgers.") As each person presents his/her statements, the other group members try to guess which one of the statements was false. After they guess, the person reveals which one was false and the next person takes a turn.

C.   GROUP RULES

Have the group brainstorm rules for how they want to treat one another in group. Write the rules on a sheet of newsprint and then have all group members sign the paper as their commitment to these rules. Be sure that the rules are posted each week during meetings.

Be sure the following guidelines are included:
- ◆ **No put-downs or name calling**
- ◆ **Take turns talking**
- ◆ **Confidentiality** – Give examples. Be sure to add that the adults must break this confidentiality if they feel that a child is being hurt, physically or sexually, or if there is a concern that a child is going to hurt him/herself.

LEARNING ACTIVITIES

A.   REASONS TO BE ANGRY

 20 min.

Ask the group to come up with a list of all the reasons that someone can feel angry and record their responses on a flipchart. Remind the group that there are no right or wrong answers.

B. WAYS TO REACT

Say to the group, "There are many different ways people react when they're angry-- both positive and negative. What are some of those ways?"

Have the participants tell the group different ways people react when they are angry. Record their answers on a new flipchart sheet.

Tell the group that for the next 11 weeks, they will focus on positive ways to react when they feel angry so that they can feel good about themselves instead of having a situation go from bad to worse.

C. WHEN I GET MAD I...

Distribute a "When I get mad I..." worksheet to each participant. Ask group members to fill out the sheet, checking the appropriate box, being as honest as possible. Depending upon the group's reading level, the leader may need to assist.

Instruct the participants to put their names on their worksheets. Collect and hold onto each group member's checklist until the end of the 12 sessions together. Participants will fill out the same sheet again at the closing of the last session so they can evaluate their improvement.

CLOSING ACTIVITY

 5 min.

BOPPITY BOP BOP BOP

Have everyone stand in a circle with one person in the middle.

The person in the middle points to someone around the circle and says "Boppity Bop Bop Bop" as fast as s/he can. By the time this person finishes saying that phrase, the person who is pointed at has to say "Bop." If that person says it too late or not at all, s/he goes in the middle.

The person in the middle also has the option to just say "Bop" to someone. In that case, the person pointed at can't say anything at all or s/he goes in the middle.

The person in the middle does not need to go around the circle in order.

1. If the group has difficulty focusing and listening, develop a "Peace Stick" for the group to use each week. The rule of the Peace Stick is that the only person allowed to talk is the person holding the Peace Stick.

2. Keep a folder for each participant. Everything that group members complete throughout the 12 sessions should be compiled in their individual folders and handed back to them during the last meeting. The leaders can write progress notes in the folders as well.

When I get mad I...

Check the right box for you:

	Always	Some-times	Never
1. Hit or kick the person.....................			
2. Ignore the person........................			
3. Take a deep breath and relax.........			
4. Listen to the person I'm mad at.......			
5. Call him/her a name back.............			
6. Threaten him/her.........................			
7. Tease others...............................			
8. Find a safe teacher, parent, or adult			
9. Stop and think before I react..........			

DISCOVERING MY ANGER
SESSION TWO

LESSON OBJECTIVES

⇒ Continue to build trust within the group.

⇒ Recognize how anger is triggered in different ways and to varying degrees.

⇒ Identify the physical sensations of anger.

SUPPLIES NEEDED

☑ Markers, colored pencils and/or crayons

☑ One copy of "I get angry when…" list

☑ Copies of "Yes" and "No" supplement

☑ Copies of "This is how I feel when I'm angry" worksheet, or

☑ Copies of "What does your anger feel like?" worksheet ★

☑ A die

BEFORE THE MEETING

Read the lesson and select activity options that are age appropriate for your group. Collect necessary supplies. Prior to the meeting, make enough copies of the "Yes and "No" supplement so that each group member has a Yes and a No card.

NOTES TO THE LEADER

Most of the time, we're only asked about our anger after we're already mad, and usually, that is a difficult time to communicate how we're feeling. The purpose of this session is for group members to begin thinking about their anger more objectively (when they aren't necessarily in the midst of an angering situation).

After this lesson, participants will be able to understand and define better what makes them angry and recognize how their body feels and reacts when their anger is triggered.

10 min.

A. MEMORY TEST

Before passing out the name-tents from last week, challenge the group to remember everyone's names, what they drew, and what was said about themselves from their name-tents. Hand out the name-tents.

If there are any new group members, be sure that they are given an opportunity to create a name-tent.

B. RULES REVIEW

Ask group members to review the group rules that were developed during the last session. Post the rules for everyone to see.

LEARNING ACTIVITIES

 10 min.

A. I GET ANGRY WHEN...

Distribute a "Yes" and "No" card to each participant. One at a time, slowly read the statements from the "I get angry when…" list. Each person should hold up a "Yes" or "No" card following each statement, according to whether s/he gets angry in that particular situation or not. If the statement does not pertain to someone in the group, that person should not put up either card. (Example: The facilitator says, "My sister or brother teases me," and someone in the group is an only child.)

Emphasize the importance of not laughing at others or commenting on anybody else's card. Also, stress the value of everyone having their own feelings, experiences, and opinions, which are not necessarily those of their peers. In other words, remind them to *think for themselves*.

Follow-up Discussion

- What do you think was the purpose of this activity? (To recognize that anger is triggered by many different things.)

- Can you think of other situations that trigger your anger?

- What causes us to get angry at some things and not angry at other things?

- Is it okay for us to feel angry? Why or why not?

- Is it okay to handle our anger any way that we feel? Why or why not?

- Do all situations make you feel the same amount of anger? Why or why not?

B. THIS IS HOW I FEEL WHEN I'M ANGRY

20 min.

Using the "This is how I feel when I'm angry" worksheet, ask the group to draw what they *feel* like when they're angry. Emphasize that the picture does not need to look like them, but should reflect how they feel. (Examples: a firecracker because she feels like she's going to explode, or his body on fire because he feels really hot when he's mad.)

After they are finished drawing, have the participants show their drawings to the group and talk about them.

- OR -

WHAT DOES YOUR ANGER LOOK LIKE? ★

10 min.

Hand out a "What does your anger look like?" worksheet and markers/colored pencils to each person. Ask the participants to draw what their body parts feel like when they're angry. They may choose to draw the body parts randomly on the page or fit them into a whole body. To help them with this exercise, encourage the participants to think back and remember how their bodies felt sometime when they were particularly angry.

After they are finished drawing, have the participants show their drawings to the group and talk about them.

C. ROLL THE DIE

Go around the circle and have group members take turns rolling a die. According to whichever number is turned up, the person answers the question below:

1 - Who is a safe person you can turn to when you're mad?
2 - How can you tell when a close friend is mad at you?
3 - What is something you can do to cool off when you're mad?
4 - In what ways do you think anger can be helpful/useful?
5 - Describe a time when you've reacted negatively while feeling angry and later regretted it?
6 - What is one thing that you want to get out of this group?

CLOSING ACTIVITY

 5 min.

COMFORT RATING

On the count of three, ask participants to rate with their fingers, from one through five, how comfortable they are feeling in the group so far. (1 being not at all comfortable, 5 being extremely comfortable).

HELPFUL HINTS

If you have a group with young participants who are having difficulty focusing or following rules, you may want to give out stickers, stars, or small candies to group members who are doing what they should be doing for positive reinforcement.

I GET ANGRY WHEN...

1. I GET TEASED ABOUT SOMETHING I AM WEARING.
2. PEOPLE TALK MEANLY ABOUT MY MOM.
3. MY PARENTS FIGHT.
4. A PET DIES.
5. NO ONE SEEMS TO CARE ABOUT ME.
6. MY TEACHER YELLS AT ME.
7. I HAVE TO GO TO A NEW SCHOOL.
8. I FEEL LEFT OUT.
9. SOMEONE TELLS ME THAT I AM UGLY.
10. I HAVE TO DO SOMETHING THAT I DON'T WANT TO DO.
11. I GET HIT.
12. I FEEL LIKE I DON'T GET TO MAKE MY OWN DECISIONS.
13. I DON'T DO SOMETHING WELL.
14. MY SISTER OR BROTHER TEASES ME.
15. SOMEONE CLOSE TO ME DIES.
16. SOMEONE I LOVE DRINKS TOO MUCH ALCOHOL OR USES DRUGS.
17. I FEEL EMBARRASSED ABOUT MY FAMILY.
18. I DON'T FEEL SMART.
19. I DON'T FEEL LISTENED TO.
20. I'M NOT GETTING THE ATTENTION THAT I NEED.
21. I DON'T SEE MY DAD.
22. I DON'T SEE MY MOM.
23. SOMEONE CAUSES ME TO CRY.
24. I FEEL LIKE I DON'T HAVE ANY FRIENDS.
25. I GET EMBARRASSED.
26. THERE'S NOTHING TO DO AFTER SCHOOL.
27. I HAVE TO GO AND LIVE WITH A NEW FAMILY.
28. I WORK HARD ON SOMETHING AND NO ONE NOTICES.
29. WHEN PEOPLE TALK ABOUT ME BEHIND MY BACK.
30. WHEN SOMEONE MESSES WITH ME.

Prior to the session, make enough copies for each participant to have a "Yes" and a "No" card. Cut the cards into slips for group members to hold up during the "I get angry when…" learning activity.

YES	NO
YES	NO
YES	NO
YES	NO
YES	NO

This is how I feel when I'm angry:

What does your ANGER feel like?

What do your body parts feel like when you're angry?

eyes

mouth

hands/arms

hair

feet/legs

blood

heart

stomach

voice

head

"BUT IT WASN'T MY FAULT!"
SESSION THREE

LESSON OBJECTIVES

⇒ Recognize the importance of taking responsibility for our mistakes.

⇒ Learn and practice the skill of owning up to our errors.

⇒ Develop trust and build group cohesion.

SUPPLIES NEEDED

☑ Check-in cube

☑ Marshmallows

☑ Toothpicks

☑ Markers

☑ One copy of "I will not fight with you today" poem or

☑ One copy of "Autobiography in Five Short Chapters" poem ★

BEFORE THE MEETING

Read the lesson and select activity options that are age-appropriate for the group. Collect the supplies. Using an empty square box, make a cube with a different question from the warm-up activity written on each side of the cube.

NOTES TO THE LEADER

A challenging skill for many of us to learn is how to take responsibility for our mistakes. It feels easier to just pass the blame onto someone else or to justify our negative actions, but that doesn't usually help us in the long run.

In this session, we'll help the group members explore the impact of owning up their mistakes, and in turn, make them more trustworthy. This is an important skill in peacemaking because they can only learn and change if they're able to recognize and accept their mistakes.

MEETING WARM-UP

C. RULES REVIEW

Briefly review the group rules developed during the first session and post them for everyone to see.

B. ROLL 'EM!

 10 min.

Using the square box, instruct participants to take turns rolling the cube and reading and answering aloud the question that is face up.

Suggestions For Cube Questions

- Name a high (good thing) and a low (not-so-good thing) from your past week.

- Tell something about yourself that no one else here knows.

- Describe a time that you felt very angry but controlled yourself.

- What is something that you really like about your family?

- What's one thing that you like to do on weekends?

- What is something that often makes you feel very angry?

LEARNING ACTIVITIES

A. BUT IT WASN'T ME!

 10 min.

Ask for a couple of volunteers to help you with a role-play demonstration. Instruct your helpers to pretend they're talking in class and to deny responsibility when they're reprimanded. Begin "teaching." When your volunteers start talking, ask them to be quiet. They should deny any responsibility, saying, "It wasn't me. I wasn't talking." Do this a couple of times.

Then, instruct the pair to stop talking, and have another couple of group members pretend to talk to one another. Begin "teaching" again. When the second pair of volunteers begin talking, you (the teacher) should turn around and yell at the first pair (who were talking before, but not this time.) They will likely rebuttal and say, "It wasn't us! We weren't talking! It was them!"

Ask the group, "Is the teacher likely to believe them? Why or why not?"

Follow-up Discussion

- It can be extremely frustrating and angering to be blamed for something that you didn't do. What is a positive way to handle a situation when you're blamed for something that you didn't do? How could you let someone know the truth without getting so angry that you lose control?

- In this situation, why didn't I, as the teacher, believe the students when they said they weren't talking the second time? Do you think the result could have been different if the students took responsibility from the beginning? Why or why not?

- Why do you think it's important to take responsibility when you mess up? What can happen as a result of being honest? What can happen as a result of being dishonest?

- If someone sees you take responsibility when you do mess up, is s/he more likely to believe you in future situations? Why or why not?

B. MARSHMALLOW MADNESS

 20 min.

Using marshmallows, toothpicks, and markers, ask each group member to create a "person" or two out of marshmallows.

Divide the group into pairs and ask each pair to develop a realistic situation, using their marshmallow characters, in which they take responsibility for their actions rather than passing the blame onto someone else.

Each pair should present their role-play to the group.

CLOSING ACTIVITY

 5 min.

"AUTOBIOGRAPHY IN FIVE SHORT CHAPTERS" ★

Read aloud "Autobiography in Five Short Chapters" by Portia Nelson. Ask the group how this poem relates to today's theme of taking responsibility.

- OR -

"I WILL NOT FIGHT WITH YOU TODAY"

Read aloud the poem "I will not fight with you today." Challenge group members to memorize it and remember it for next week.

HELPFUL HINTS

The leftover marshmallows can be a great group snack!

Autobiography In Five Short Chapters

BY PORTIA NELSON

I.

I walk down the street.
There is a deep hole in the sidewalk.
I fall in
I am lost…I am helpless.
It isn't my fault.
It takes forever to find a way out.

II.

I walk down the same street.
There is a deep hole in the sidewalk.
I pretend I don't see it.
I fall in again.
I can't believe I'm in the same place,
But, it isn't my fault.
It still takes a long time to get out.

III.

I walk down the same street.
There is a deep hole in the sidewalk.
I see it is there.
I still fall in… it's a habit.
My eyes are open.
I know where I am.
It is my fault.
I get out immediately.

IV.

I walk down the same street.
There is a deep hole in the sidewalk.
I walk around it.

V.

I walk down another street.

I will not fight with you today

I will not fight with you today,

No I won't, I'll only say,

"I do feel mad, that's okay,

We'll work it out another way."

If I feel my anger rise,

I'll push the urge to hurt aside.

I can think and use my mind,

And leave all violence far behind.

WARNING: I'M GETTING MAD!

SESSION FOUR

LESSON OBJECTIVES

⇒ Learn to recognize our internal anger warning signs before it's too late and we lose control.

⇒ Personally identify one positive and healthy way each group member can use to keep from losing control.

⇒ Continue to build group cohesion and encourage sharing.

SUPPLIES NEEDED

☑ Eight playing cards, numbers 2 – 9

☑ One copy of "Warning Cards" supplement

☑ Clay

☑ Paper and pen for facilitator

☑ Small object to pass (like a ball or bean bag)

BEFORE THE MEETING

Read the lesson and gather supplies. Copy and cut out the warning cards for Activity A.

NOTES TO THE LEADER

Sometimes our anger can spiral out of control almost before we even recognize we're mad. For example, someone may pick up a chair and throw it across the room before even thinking about what s/he is doing. People who do such things may tell you that they felt completely out of control and couldn't help it. However, they *can* and *should* control themselves.

This session will help group members recognize their own internal warning signs when they're angry, so that they can more easily prevent their anger from getting out of control. Each group member will also come up with a personal way to cool off once s/he notices a warning sign.

DECK OF SHARING

10 min.

Spread out eight playing cards (numbers 2 through 9) on the table face down. One at a time, ask each group member to select a card and answer the following question depending upon his/her card number:

2 – What has been the best part of your day 2-day?

3 – Name **3** of your favorite foods.

4 – On a typical night, what do you usually do be-**4** dinner?

5 – Share a memory from when you were **5** years old?

6 – How do you want to spend your 16th birthday?

7 – If you were given $7.00 to spend today, how would you spend it?

8 – Do you like to sk+8? Roller sk+8 or ice sk+8?

9 – What are you normally doing at **9:00** p.m. on a school night?

LEARNING ACTIVITIES

A. WARNING CARDS

10 min.

Say to the group, "Feeling angry is just another feeling, like feeling sad, happy, excited, or bored. You can't help feeling mad, and although it doesn't feel good, anger is as normal as any other feeling. It's our reaction to our anger that often results in situations going from bad to worse. The key is to prevent our anger from taking over by recognizing it before it's too late."

⇒ What are your warning signs that you are about to lose control?

Using the set of warning cards you have copied and cut out, lay the cards face up around the table or floor. Ask group members, one at a time, to choose two or three of the cards that best name the internal warning signs they experience when they feel like they could lose control.

After a group member has finished telling the group the warning signs s/he picked, s/he should return the cards so the next person can have the option to use them.

⇒ How can knowing your warning signs be helpful to you?

B. CLAY PLAY

 20 min.

Distribute a small amount of clay to each group member.

Be sure to emphasize to them that it's okay to feel angry. Say: "What we are working on are helpful and healthy ways to deal with our anger, not taking away the anger or stuffing it."

Ask group members to each sculpt one positive and healthy way to keep from losing control when feeling angry. (Examples: A shoe because I want to walk away from the situation. A brain because I want to think before I say something I'll regret.)

Ask the participants to take turns showing and talking about their sculptures with the group. After everyone is finished sharing, ask:

- What other positive things can you do with all of that energy you've created in being mad? (Examples: run around the block, punch a pillow, cry, call a friend.)

- How can you let a person know you're mad without name-calling or making a situation worse? (Examples: tell him/her in a calm voice that you feel angry, state your feelings.)

- If the method you created from your clay doesn't work, what's something else you could do? It's always good to have at least two or three methods you can try, because the first try doesn't always work.

CLOSING ACTIVITY

SECRET PASS

5 min.

Instruct the group to stand in a close circle with their hands behind them. Select a person to be in the middle. Using a small object, those in the circle secretly pass the object around the outside of the circle and the person in the middle tries to guess who is holding the object. The people around the circle should pretend that they have the object, even when they don't. After the person in the middle guesses who is the correct person holding the object, that person goes into the middle.

WARNING CARDS Cut out the following common anger warning signs. Have each participant identify two or three personal warning signs that s/he is about to lose control.

Feel hot	**Rush of energy**
Can't think clearly	**Want to scream**
Want to get away from everyone	**Feel like hurting the person**
Feel like crying	**Want to make the other person feel bad**
Stomach turns or knots up	**Head pounds**
Can't get my mind off of it	**OTHER (not on cards)**

DIGGING DEEPER: WHAT'S UNDER ALL THAT ANGER?

SESSION FIVE

LESSON OBJECTIVES

⇒ Demonstrate how we cover up other feelings with our anger.

⇒ Explore and identify which "core feelings" we most often mask with our anger.

SUPPLIES NEEDED

☑ One copy of "Core Feeling Cards" supplement

☑ Paper plate and crayons, or

☑ Copies of "Underneath my anger I feel" worksheet ★

BEFORE THE MEETING

Read the lesson, select age-appropriate activities, and gather supplies. Using a paper plate and crayons, draw an angry facial expression on the plate to be used during Learning Activity A for younger children.

Also, make a copy and cut out the Core Feeling Cards for Learning Activity B.

NOTES TO THE LEADER

This session helps participants recognize other feelings that are often masked or covered up by anger. Acknowledging these other feelings can help us understand why we may feel angry so much, when in fact, we are feeling many other things, but transferring it into anger because it's easier to feel.

This session also encourages a deeper level of sharing. Be sure to remind the group about the importance of confidentiality.

⏳ 5 min.

WOULD YOU RATHER?

Read the following "Would you rather" statements to the participants. Group members who would rather do the first of the two choices should hold up a thumb. Those who would rather do the second thing should hold a thumb down. They must decide one or the other. Encourage them to think for themselves and not just do what everyone else is doing.

Ask the group: "Would you rather…"

1. …Go to the movies on a beautiful, sunny day OR go swimming on a cool, cloudy day?
2. …Play a sport OR watch a sport?
3. …Be given $10,000 OR earn $100,000?
4. …Eat at Kentucky Fried Chicken OR McDonald's?
5. …Be the only child OR have ten sisters and brothers?
6. …Read a book OR do math problems?
7. …Have a lot of friends that you don't know very well OR have only one very close friend.
8. …Be too hot OR be too cold?
9. …Be lost in the jungle OR lost in the desert?
10. …Sleep in until noon OR stay up all night?

LEARNING ACTIVITIES

A. CORE FEELING CARDS

⏳ 5 min.

Continuing with the Warm-up activity, ask the group:

- Would you rather feel angry OR would you rather feel sad?

- Would you rather feel angry OR would you rather feel jealous?

- Would you rather feel angry OR would you rather feel hurt?

Say: "Feeling sad, jealous, or hurt can be very painful. These are difficult feelings to have. Most of us would prefer to feel angry over these other feelings because anger is less painful. Often times we mask, or cover up, these harder feelings with anger. For example, when someone calls you a name that hurts your feelings, you're actually feeling *hurt*, but you might turn that hurt into anger because it's easier to feel angry than it is to feel hurt."

Using the paper plate with the angry face drawn on it, demonstrate how people mask their anger. Whisper to a volunteer to say something to you (just for pretend) that would likely hurt your feelings. After the volunteer says it to you in front of the group, put the paper plate in front of your face to demonstrate how you covered your core feeling of hurt with anger. Do this with several different group members, using core feelings such as sad, disappointed, jealous, etc.

- OR -

UNDERNEATH MY ANGER I FEEL… ★

Pass out the worksheet, "Underneath my anger I feel…" and ask the participants to color in the body according to what they feel underneath their anger. Allow time for each group member to talk about his/her drawings with the rest of the group.

B. CARD PICK

 15 min.

Using the Core Feeling cards, place the cards face down on the table so no one can read them. Instruct group members to take turns picking a Core Feeling card. The person who picks the card acts out the feeling while the rest of the group tries to guess which feeling it is. They should be encouraged to use words and real life examples from times when they've actually felt the emotions to help them be more convincing and make it easier to guess.

CLOSING ACTIVITY

15 min.

YOU PICK 'EM!

Set the Core Feeling cards face up on the table and instruct group members to, one at a time, choose two core hurts they most often cover up with their anger. Ask them to give an example of an experience they've had with each core feeling they chose. (Example: "I picked jealous because I get jealous or mad of other kids who live with both of their parents.") They should return their cards immediately after they've shared so the next person can choose the same card if s/he wants.

Core Feeling Cards

Sad	Hurt
Scared	Jealous
Worried	Confused
Disappointed	Bored
Overwhelmed	Unimportant (or ignored)
Embarrassed	Other (not on cards)

Underneath my anger, I feel . . .

jealous = green

sad = yellow

scared = red

embarrassed = blue

hurt = brown

lonely = purple

worried = orange

other feeling = black

Color the person where you most often feel the emotion.

WE ARE PEACEMAKERS

SESSION SIX

LESSON OBJECTIVES

⇒ Express positive and creative problem-solving skills.

⇒ Introduce the concept that we are all peacemakers.

SUPPLIES NEEDED

- ☑ Small ball of yarn or string
- ☑ Copies of "Cartoon Creation" worksheet
- ☑ Pencils, colored pencils, crayons, and/or markers
- ☑ Chalkboard, flipchart paper, or other large sheets of paper

BEFORE THE MEETING

Read the lesson plan and choose appropriate activities for your group. Collect necessary supplies.

NOTES TO THE LEADER

In this session, group members will create a realistic scenario of a time when they lost control of their anger. They will draw the scenario in a comic strip format, but re-create the ending, using peacemaking skills such as talking it out, ignoring the person, or telling a teacher. This activity promotes problem solving and creativity.

MEETING WARM-UP

 5 min.

STRING TOSS

Standing in a circle, toss a ball of string or yarn across the circle to a group member, while holding onto the end of the string. Ask the person who catches the ball, "What was something fun you did this past week?" After the person answers, s/he should toss the ball to another group member, while holding onto a piece of the string, and ask the person receiving the ball of yarn the same question.

Eventually, your circle should look like a web, signifying how the group is connected.

LEARNING ACTIVITIES

 15 min.

A. CARTOON CREATION

Distribute a copy of the "Cartoon Creation" worksheet to each group member. Ask them to create a comic strip that depicts a personal situation in which s/he got really angry and reacted in a way s/he later regretted. But instead of drawing the original negative ending, ask participants to recreate a new ending that demonstrates a positive result of the situation.

The cartoon should have a beginning, middle, and end, and everyone should have an opportunity to show and explain their cartoons to the group.

Collect their cartoons and place them in participants' individual folders to return to them later, after the final group meeting.

 15 min.

B. PEACEMAKERS

Say to the group: "As we begin to think about ways we can control our anger and make situations better instead of worse, we become peacemakers. We are all peacemakers. You now know what triggers your anger and what your personal warning signs are when you feel mad. Now it's time for us to really explore the many different ways to let our feelings out, but at the same time keep control."

On the top of a sheet of flipchart paper or chalkboard, write the heading, "I am a peacemaker when… " Ask the group to come up with suggestions of what it means to be a peacemaker. Write their suggestions on the flipchart. Help them to recognize that they, too, are peacemakers because they are working toward solving their problems peacefully and not hurting other people's feelings or bodies.

Keep the list they make and post it prior to the next meeting.

CLOSING ACTIVITY

 5 min.

GROUP AFFIRMATION

Take turns going around the circle, with each person saying one thing s/he appreciates or likes about this group.

Cartoon Creation

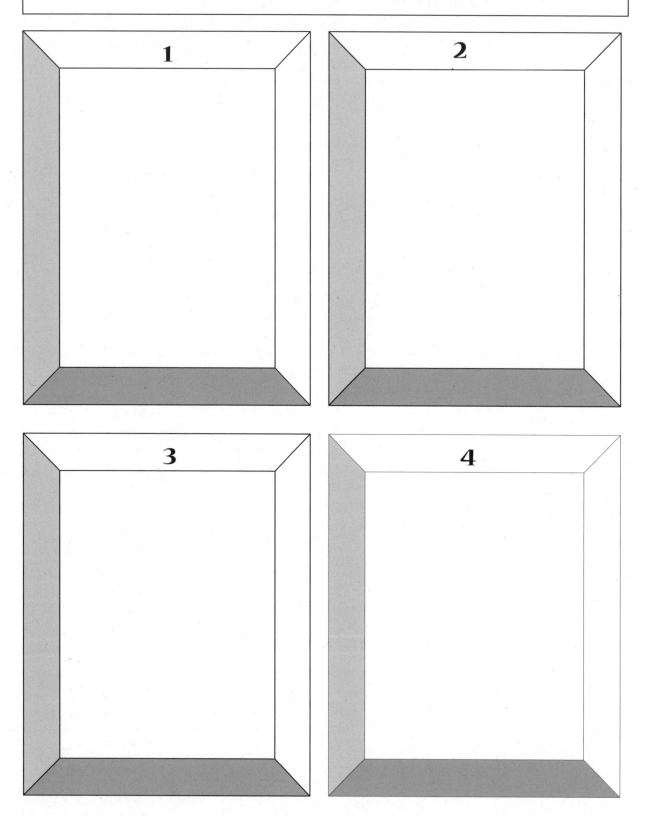

KEEP YOUR PERSONAL POWER

SESSION SEVEN

LESSON OBJECTIVES

⇒ Discern how people provoke our anger as a means of control.

⇒ Problem-solve positive approaches to "real life" situations.

⇒ Learn five key steps to processing and controlling our anger.

SUPPLIES NEEDED

☑ Pencils

☑ Role Play Scenarios ★

☑ Finger puppets (or several small stuffed animals) for younger children

☑ Copies of "5 steps to controlling your anger" worksheet

BEFORE THE MEETING

Read the lesson, gather necessary supplies, and select age-appropriate activities for your group. If using the role-play scenarios, copy and cut the scenarios into slips prior to the meeting.

NOTES TO THE LEADER

Today's lesson is important in understanding the exchange of power or control that occurs when someone intentionally "tries to make you mad." The session demonstrates how sometimes people say or do things hoping to elicit an angry reaction from an other person, and when that person reacts as expected, the reactive person gives up his/her personal power or control. In other words, don't give the person the satisfaction by reacting how they want you to.

This concept may be a little complicated for younger participants, and a more simplified explanation of the same theme can be given to them.

The group will also learn healthy and helpful techniques for handling such situations.

10 min.

I'VE GOT MAIL FOR...

Participants should sit in their chairs in an open circle with no empty chairs. A volunteer stands in the middle. The goal of the person in the middle is to get out of the middle and find an open seat. S/he says, "I've got mail for...," and finishes off the statement with something like, "everyone who lives in an apartment." Everyone who lives in an apartment then gets up and runs to a different open chair. Meanwhile, the person in the middle finds an open chair and sits down. (Those who do not live in an apartment remain seated.) No one can go back to the same chair within the same round. The person left standing without a chair is now in the middle and says a different "I've got mail for..." statement.

LEARNING ACTIVITIES

A. ROLE-PLAY SCENARIOS ★

 20 min.

Say to the group, "Sometimes people hurt our feelings by accident. But other times, people hurt our feelings on purpose because they want to provoke us and see us get angry. For example, if they say to you, 'You're nasty and you look like a dog,' they're not looking to make a friend, but they're looking to make you angry. If you give them the reaction they expect, you give them the power and they 'win.' But if you refuse to react the way they want or expect, you keep your personal power. It's important that you learn to control your initial reaction of lashing back at them."

Using the scenarios provided as a supplement, split the group into threes and have them act out the situations, developing a result in which the person who gets angry maintains his/her personal power and doesn't do what the "provoker" hopes or expects.

Give each group member an opportunity to play the role of the "provoker" and the "defender."

Follow-up Discussion

- Why does someone talk about someone else's mom or tell a person that they are poor or smell nasty? (To get someone mad.)

- And if you give someone the reaction that they want, who is in control? (They are)

- When you chose to ignore the person or pretend not to be angry, who is in control then? (You are)

- Why does it sometimes make us feel good to pick on others?

- OR-

FINGER PUPPET PLAY

If the participants are too young to read and act out the role-play scenarios on their own, use finger puppets (or small stuffed animals) to role-play the scenario situations for the entire group. Get the kids involved in the acting out of the finger puppets and in creating positive solutions.

 10 min.

B. 5 STEPS TO CONTROLLING YOUR ANGER

Distribute the "5 steps to controlling your anger" worksheet to each group member. Instruct group members to link each step with the appropriate picture.

(NOTE: If you feel your group is too advanced for this worksheet, hand out blank pieces of paper and ask that each person develop his/her personal 5-step plan.)

Follow-up Discussion

- How can these steps be useful when someone is provoking you?

- Remember, feeling angry is okay and it's important to talk about it and not to stuff your anger inside. However, you don't need to react immediately or react to the "provoker" directly. If someone has made you really mad, but you don't want him/her to have the satisfaction of knowing it, who is someone else you can turn to or talk to about it?

- How can you best remember these 5 steps?

CLOSING ACTIVITY

MEMORY CONTEST

 5 min.

Collect the "5 steps" worksheets so no one can see them. Have a contest to see who can remember all 5 steps in the correct order. Tell participants that they should remember the steps for next week because you will ask the group to recall them.

ROLE-PLAY SCENARIOS: Using the following scenarios, ask pairs or groups of three to develop a positive and healthy response to their scenario. Encourage the chosen "provoker" of the scenario to be persistent and not give up, and encourage the "defender" to avoid giving into what the "provoker" expects or wants.

Scenario #1:

A classmate continues to say disrespectful things about your mom.

Scenario #2:

You are on the bus minding your own business and a kid two grades older than you tells you you're poor because of the street you live on. You're not allowed to move seats and the kid won't stop harassing you.

Scenario #3:

You're at home watching your all-time favorite television show. Your older sibling walks up and grabs the remote control without asking and changes the channel, laughing as s/he does it. No adult is at home at the time.

Scenario #4:

You are sitting in your seat in class and the person next to you keeps looking at you and rolls his or her eyes at you. S/he then breathes in your face. It's obvious s/he is doing it on purpose.

Scenario #5:

After lunch you go back to your classroom and open your desk or locker. You discover that your watch is missing and you're sure you left your watch there before lunch. Two kids walk by and snicker, like they may know what's going on.

Scenario #6

You and a friend are talking in class. The teacher has asked you twice to be quiet. This time, it's your friend who talks, but the teacher asks only you to leave and go to the office.

Five Steps to controlling your ANGER

Which Steps go with each picture?

1. **Realize and accept that you're angry.**
2. **Count to 10 and breathe deeply.**
3. **Think of something peaceful to help calm you down.**
4. **Think about what may happen if you lose control.**
5. **Do something positive with your anger instead.**

_____

_____

I am so mad right now!

_____

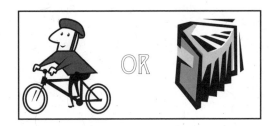

OR

_____

=

_____

IT'S ALL IN *HOW* YOU SAY IT

SESSION EIGHT

LESSON OBJECTIVES

⇒ Further develop creative, problem-solving skills during difficult situations.

⇒ Empower group members as peacemakers.

⇒ Practice diffusing situations through what we say and how we say it.

SUPPLIES NEEDED

☑ Reference to "5 steps to controlling your anger" from prior session

☑ One copy of "Dear Peacemakers" letter

☑ One copy of "Helpful Comebacks" supplement

☑ Piece of paper

☑ Slips of paper and pencils

BEFORE THE MEETING

Prior to the start of your meeting, copy the "Helpful Comebacks" supplement and cut the "Insults" (💣) and "Helpful Comebacks" (✌) into slips for Learning Activity B.

NOTES TO THE LEADER

When being provoked or harassed by someone, ignoring the person or finding a safe adult doesn't always work. Although those are good options, sometimes there isn't an adult around, or ignoring the person isn't proving effective. In these instances, it may necessary to deal with the situation head on and by yourself.

In this session, group members will use their creative ideas, knowledge and problem-solving skills to uncover ways to hold on to their personal pride ("save face"), while also avoiding making a situation worse.

5 min.

MEMORY CONTEST II

Challenge the group to recall the "5 steps to controlling your anger" from the last session. After the "5 steps" are again fresh in their minds, move on to the first learning activity.

LEARNING ACTIVITIES

10 min.

A. "DEAR PEACEMAKERS" LETTER

Ask a volunteer to read aloud the letter from Angry & Alone. Using the skills and knowledge that the group has gained from prior sessions, ask the group to give helpful, positive advice to Angry & Alone.

The group can verbally brainstorm ideas for what Angry & Alone should do. Another option is for each person to write Angry & Alone a letter back with helpful advice, or the group could take turns role-playing the situation, developing a variety of positive choices.

20 min.

B. HELPFUL COMEBACKS

This activity is similar to the prior session's role-playing scenarios, except instead of role-playing an entire scenario, group members will need to practice using their words sincerely, without sounding snide, in order to diffuse a situation.

Using the "Helpful Come-Backs" slips, hand out a written insult to a group member (from the side with the 💣 symbol). This person should read his/her insult to his/her partner, sounding as realistic as possible. The person receiving the insult needs to come up with something to say back that doesn't escalate or make the situation worse. If the person receiving the insult has difficulty coming up with something to say that diffuses the situation, give him/her the slip with the corresponding number (from the side with the ✌ symbol) to say.

This is a great activity for emphasizing the importance of *how* we say things, and to practice saying things without "an attitude." Have the rest of the group rate the person from 1 to 5 as to how well s/he defuses the insult and whether or not they hear "an attitude." Allow an opportunity for group members to play each role.

5 min.

WRITE IT OUT

Pass out two slips of paper and a pencil to each person. Each participant should write down two ways (one on each slip) s/he can demonstrate to his/her classroom and friends that s/he is a peacemaker. When they're finished, collect the slips, mix them up, and hand out two to each group member for him/her to read aloud to the group. (They will most likely be reading each other's suggestions and not their own.)

Dear Peacemakers,

Yesterday during lunch I was sitting at a table eating my sandwich. I got up to get more milk and when I returned, someone had moved my lunch to another table. Some other person was sitting in my seat! I felt so angry! I also felt sad and unimportant, like no one liked me.

What should I do, peacemakers? Please help me!

Your friend,
Angry & Alone

Helpful Comebacks

WHAT SOMEONE MAY SAY TO YOU:	WHAT YOU COULD SAY BACK: (without an "attitude")
1. "Your Momma!"	1. "That's odd because I don't think you even know my Momma!"
2. "You're so ugly!"	2. "I like the way I look, thank you."
3. "You smell."	3. "That's funny, I just took a bath last night."
4. "That is so gay."	4. "Are you trying to hurt my feelings?"
5. "Get away, you can't be in our group."	5. "Why are you so mad at me?"
6. "I don't want to be your partner."	6. "I'm sorry to hear that."
7. "I bet I did better on that test than you did."	7. "Well then, congratulations."
8. "Get away from me."	8. "Why don't you want to be near me? Are you mad at me or something?"
9. "You always make us lose."	9. "I'm trying to do the best that I can. I'm sorry you feel that way."
10. "You live in a trash can."	10. "Actually, I don't. That's nice that you care so much about where I live though."

CREATING POSITIVE CHANGE
SESSION NINE

LESSON OBJECTIVES

⇒ Practice stating your feelings and what you want from another person.

⇒ Explore how family members express their anger and how that can influence your own expression of anger.

SUPPLIES NEEDED

☑ Package of Starburst brand candy

☑ One copy of "I'm Feeling _____ because…" supplement

☑ Copies of "Family Anger" worksheet

☑ Pencils

BEFORE THE MEETING

Prior to the start of your meeting, make a copy of the "I'm Feeling _____ because…" supplement and cut it into slips (enough for each group member to have one).

NOTES TO THE LEADER

In today's session, group members will practice stating what they're feeling when they're angry, why they're feeling that way, and what they want the people they're angry with to change.

Also in this lesson, group members will explore the various ways their families express anger and how that can influence their own expression of anger.

⌛ 10 min.

STARBURST FUN

Instruct the group, one at a time, to select a Starburst candy from the bag (without looking). Depending upon the color the person picks, s/he should answer the following questions:

Strawberry: If you could have dinner with any famous person, who would you choose?

Cherry: How do you think your school could be a safer place for students?

Orange: What's a high point (a good thing) and a low point (a bad thing) from your past week?

Lemon: What is one thing you've learned from being in this group?

LEARNING ACTIVITIES

⌛ 15 min.

A. I'M FEELING _____ BECAUSE...

One at a time, ask each group member to recall a time within the past week that s/he got mad. After explaining his/her story, ask him/her to say the following statement, using the particular situation.

"I'm feeling _____ (state your feeling),

because_____ (state what happened)."

"I'd like it if _____ (state what you want to change)."

Explain to the group how using these phrases and words can be very helpful to someone and to them because it explains what they're feeling, why they feel the way they do, and what they'd like to see changed for the better.

Hand out "I'm feeling _____ because..." slips to everyone to take with them as a helpful reminder of the phrase. Encourage group members to use this phrase sometime during the week after something or someone triggered their anger.

B. FAMILY ANGER

15 min.

Say to the group: "How your family deals with their anger can have a direct effect on how you handle your own anger. Today, we're going to explore the different ways our families express their anger and what you can learn from them."

Distribute a copy of the "Family Anger" worksheet to each group member. Give participants several minutes to complete it before asking them to read their answers to the group.

CLOSING ACTIVITY

SHARE WHAT YOU KNOW

5 min.

Ask each group member to tell one way s/he can teach someone in his/her classroom about peacemaking or positive anger this week.

"I'm feeling _____(state your feeling)

because_____ (state what happened)."

"I'd like it if _____ (state what you want to change)."

— —

"I'm feeling _____(state your feeling)

because_____ (state what happened)."

"I'd like it if _____ (state what you want to change)."

— —

"I'm feeling _____(state your feeling)

because_____ (state what happened)."

"I'd like it if _____ (state what you want to change)."

— —

"I'm feeling _____(state your feeling)

because_____ (state what happened)."

"I'd like it if _____ (state what you want to change)."

— —

"I'm feeling _____(state your feeling)

because_____ (state what happened)."

"I'd like it if _____ (state what you want to change)."

— —

Family Anger

I know my family members are angry when…

Some things my family members do that make me angry are…

Some negative ways my family
members deal with their anger are…

Some positive ways my family
members deal with their anger are…

Some positive ways that I deal with my anger are…

CONSEQUENCES & BULLYING

SESSION TEN

LESSON OBJECTIVES

⇒ Explore positive and negative consequences of our choices and help group members build the skill of thinking before acting.

⇒ Develop healthy outcomes in difficult and challenging situations.

⇒ Discover the motivation and harm in the choice to bully others.

SUPPLIES NEEDED

☑ Copies of "I want to interview you!" worksheet

☑ Pencils and markers

☑ One copy of "Consequence Cards" supplement

☑ Seven pieces of construction paper with "Reactions to Bullies" phrases written on each one (see list of seven items below).

☑ Masking tape

BEFORE THE MEETING

Make copies of the "I want to interview you!" worksheet.

Make a copy of the "Consequence Cards" supplement and cut them into cards.

Write each of the following statements in large letters on a separate piece of construction paper for each one:

1. Hurt the person's feelings back

2. Find someone who's weaker than me and hurt him/her

3. Laugh it off

4. Threaten him/her

5. Talk meanly about him/her to someone else

6. Stuff my feelings

7. Other

NOTES TO THE LEADER

Every choice we make has consequences. The intent of this session is to help group members anticipate and recognize possible consequences of their actions. In other words, instead of impulsively reacting to something or someone, they will learn to stop and think about the long-term ramifications of their choices.

Many of those who are frequently bullied turn around and bully someone else, expecting that it will make them feel better. In this session, group members will also look at the motivation behind bullying and its negative long-term consequences.

MEETING WARM-UP

15 min.

I WANT TO INTERVIEW YOU!

Divide the group into pairs (pairing those who don't know each other well). Pass out the "I want to interview you!" handout to each person and have partners interview one another, asking each other questions and writing down their partner's answers.

When everyone has both asked and answered the questions, instruct the participants to tell the group three things s/he learned about his/her partner.

LEARNING ACTIVITIES

10 min.

A. WHAT ARE THE CONSEQUENCES?

Say to the group: "Every day, all day, we make choices, sometimes without even thinking about it or realizing we've made a choice. And as a result of our choices, there are always consequences. Sometimes our choices are good or healthy ones, sometimes they're neutral, and sometimes our choices are poor or unhealthy. In this next activity, we are going to practice thinking about and anticipating consequences in different situations."

Using the "Consequences Cards", have group members, one at a time, pick a card from the pile, read it aloud, and come up with two or three possible consequences that would likely come from the action printed on the card.

B. BULLYING

15 min.

Tape up around the room the "reactions to bullies" phrases that were written on construction paper prior to the session. Read the statement below and instruct group members to stand under the sign that says what s/he is most likely to do after being bullied.

Read Statement: When someone bullies me or hurts my feelings, I usually want to…"

Once they are all standing under particular signs taped to the wall, ask those under each sign to tell the group possible consequences of reacting this way after being bullied or hurt.

Say: "It's very important that you think about the consequences before you react, no matter how angry or justified you may feel. It's a very important skill we all need to learn and practice throughout our lives."

Now instruct the group under each sign to take the piece of paper off the wall and, on the back, write at least five things they could do instead, that would result in positive or neutral consequences.

When finished, ask them to read their ideas to the whole group.

NOTE: The adult facilitators may need to offer help to any group member who is alone, i.e., s/he was the only one standing under his/her sign.

Follow-up Discussion

- What are some advantages that can come from being a bully?

- What are some disadvantages that can come from being a bully?

- Are there more advantages or disadvantages to being a bully?

- Do you think you have to be a bully in order to avoid being bullied by someone else? Why or why not?

- How do you think you can stand up to someone without being hurt further?

CLOSING ACTIVITY

 5 min.

LAUGH ATTACK

In this game, group members take turns trying to make the person on his/her right laugh in fifteen seconds or less. The person on the receiving end must look at the person trying to make him/her laugh and no physical contact or whispering is allowed.

I want to interview you!

1. What is your name? _____

2. Where were you born? _____

3. If you could take a trip anywhere you wanted, where would you go?

   _____

4. What is a dream or goal you have for yourself?

   _____

5. Who is a person you admire? _____

   Why? _____

6. Would you rather own a dog or a cat? _____

   Why? _____

7. If you could change one thing about your school, what would you

   change? _____

8. What's one of your favorite books? _____

9. What's one of your favorite movies? _____

10. What's one of your favorite foods? _____

Consequence Cards

You turned off your alarm and went back to sleep. You are now late for school.	Your mom asked you to clean your room and make your bed and you did it right away.
Your little brother keeps following you around and copying everything you do. You turn around and hit him.	You always finish your homework and assignments and turn them in on time.
Your grandma repeatedly asks you to help her in the kitchen. You're watching TV and ignore her.	You find a really cool pen in the school cafeteria. You pick it up, show your friends, and keep it.
A good friend tells you something and you promise her you won't tell anybody. You keep her secret.	You're talking to a friend in class. Your teacher tells you to stop talking and you lie, telling him you weren't.
A neighbor hires you to walk his dog everyday after school. You're at the mall and don't walk the dog until 6 p.m., after your neighbor is already home.	While taking a spelling test, you have the chance to cheat. You don't know your spelling words very well, but you decide not to cheat.
A kid calls you a name that really hurts your feelings. You call him a name back and threaten to beat him up after school.	At recess, a kid comes over and asks if she can play with you and your friends. Your friends say no, but you say yes.

SPREADING THE PEACE

SESSION ELEVEN

LESSON OBJECTIVES

⇒ Develop personal list of positive things to do when feeling angry.

⇒ Generate ideas for creating peace in our world.

⇒ Prepare for the celebration at the next and final session.

SUPPLIES NEEDED

☑ Piece of paper for each group member

☑ Markers

☑ Long and wide sheet of butcher paper

☑ Paint (water colors), paint brushes, and small cups of water to clean brushes. (Optional: markers or crayons for younger participants)

BEFORE THE MEETING

Read through the lesson and collect necessary supplies. Also, provide a long table for laying out the butcher paper so participants can easily paint on it.

NOTES TO THE LEADER

This lesson focuses on peace. Not only will participants create a list of peaceful options they can use when their anger rises, but participants will also think about peace in the world and how they can impact world peace.

If you have a particularly young group, you may wish to substitute markers or crayons for paint in Learning Activity B.

MEETING WARM-UP

10 min.

ONE, TWO OR THREE!

Without telling the participants why, instruct group members to hold up a number between 1 and 3. After they've chosen a number, tell them that whichever number they chose is the number of things they have to tell the group about themselves. *And*, no one can repeat what someone else has already said (for example, only one person can tell the group that s/he has a dog).

A. TOP TEN LIST

 15 min.

Distribute a blank piece of paper and markers to group members. Have each participant write ten positive and realistic things s/he can do when s/he is feeling angry.

Examples: Talk to someone about it.

Ignore the person (if I'm being teased or bullied).

Use a positive tone when I speak.

Ride my bike or run around the block.

Draw a picture.

Stop and think about the consequences.

Find a trusting adult to help.

Take deep breaths and count to 10.

When all the group members have finished their lists, have each group member read his/her list to the group. Collect the lists and laminate them (if possible) before the next session.

OPTION: Have the group develop one Top Ten List together. Following the day's session, make enough copies for each group member to have one.

B. PEACE MURAL

 15 min.

Using a long and wide piece of butcher paper and paint, direct each group member to think of a hope that s/he has for peace in the world and how s/he can play a direct role in making that hope real. Have them paint their hope onto the paper and when they're finished, ask them to explain their painting to the group. The idea is for the group to all be working on the mural together, but bringing their own individual ideas for peace onto one, large mural.

If possible, hang the peace mural up where many people can view it.

CLOSING ACTIVITY

PARTY PREP

 5 min.

The next session is the last of 12 and there will be time set aside for a small celebration. Ask for input from participants about what special treat(s) they want for their party.

Also, verify the correct spelling of participants' names for the certificates they will be receiving.

SEEING RED CELEBRATION

SESSION TWELVE

LESSON OBJECTIVE

⇒ Recognize the improvement group members have made from the first session to now.

⇒ Evaluate the group experience and content from the previous eleven sessions.

⇒ Bring closure to the group and celebrate the group members' participation in the group.

SUPPLIES NEEDED

☑ Personalized certificate of participation for each group member

☑ Participants' laminated Top Ten List from the previous session

☑ Copies of "When I get mad I…" worksheets

☑ Participants' "When I get mad I…" worksheets that were filled out during the first session

☑ Copies of "Final Evaluation" worksheet

☑ Pencils

☑ Snack food for the party

☑ Music for the party (optional)

BEFORE THE MEETING

Laminate the Top Ten List that each group member completed during the previous session. Prepare a certificate of participation for each group member prior to the meeting. Purchase snack food for the final celebration.

For Learning Activity A, bring the participants', "When I get mad I…" worksheets that they filled out during the first session.

The focus of this final session is three-fold. First, the session will help group members recognize their progress throughout the 12 sessions that the group has been meeting. Second, participants will have an opportunity to evaluate their group experience and bring closure to the group and their individual experience. And last, participants will celebrate their group experience with a small party.

MEETING WARM-UP

 5 min.

TOP TEN REVIEW

Return the laminated Top Ten List each participant created during the previous session. Ask group members if they used any of their ideas from their list since the last meeting. If so, ask them to tell about the situation. If not, ask the participants which things from their lists they would most likely use.

Encourage group members to take their list with them and post it where they would find it helpful to have the reminders nearby. (Examples: bedroom wall, school locker, or desk.)

LEARNING ACTIVITIES

 10 min.

A. WHEN I GET MAD I…

Distribute a blank "When I get mad I…" worksheet to each group member and ask the participants to complete it. (This is the same worksheet that group members completed during the first session.)

After they've finished the worksheet, hand out the, "When I get mad I…" worksheets they filled out during the first session. Ask them to compare their two "When I get mad I…" worksheets and recognize any improvement between their prior responses and now.

 10 min.

B. FINAL EVALUATION

Distribute the "Final Evaluation" worksheet to the participants. (They do not need to write their names on the paper.) Instruct them to individually complete the evaluation, being as truthful and thorough as possible. Once group members have finished their evaluation, ask them to share a portion of their evaluation with the group.

NOTE: If the group doesn't have well-developed reading/writing skills yet, the facilitators should read the evaluation questions aloud and provide necessary assistance to group members.

C. GROUP CLOSING

10 min.

Ask each person to say one positive thing about his/her group experience.

Present each participant with a certificate that states s/he has successfully completed the Seeing Red group. (See supplemental example of a certificate.)

CLOSING ACTIVITY

PARTY TIME!

10 min.

Have a Seeing Red celebration. Provide some treats and perhaps a little music for the party.

When I get mad I...

Check the right box for you:

	Always	Sometimes	Never
1. Hit or kick the person..............			
2. Ignore the person...................			
3. Take a deep breath and relax...			
4. Listen to the person I'm mad at..			
5. Call him/her a name back.........			
6. Threaten him/her...................			
7. Tease others........................			
8. Find a safe teacher, parent, or adult..................................			
9. Stop and think before I react.....			

FINAL EVALUATION

SEEING RED

1. **Today is the last day of group.**

   I feel _____ and _____ to see it end.

2. **Two things we did in this group that I liked were:**

   1. _____

   2. _____

3. **I had many different feelings during the group. Some of the feelings I had were:**

   _____   _____

   _____   _____

4. **Some important things I learned about my anger were:**

   _____

   _____

   _____

5. Something I still wonder about related to my anger is:

_____

_____

6. Some skills I learned in order to control my anger are:

_____

_____

7. I plan to continue showing I'm a peacemaker by:

_____

_____

_____

Certificate Of Participation

_____

is recognized for participating in the
SEEING RED group

_____
Name

_____
Date

Family & Children's Service

Building Strong Families, Vital Communities, and Capable Children

Family & Children's Service is a private, non-profit agency, located in Minneapolis, Minnesota. Since 1878 the agency has been working to strengthen families and communities in all their various forms. The work of Family & Children's Service encompasses the areas of mental health counseling, family and community initiatives, domestic violence prevention and intervention, public policy advocacy, family life education, and other initiatives designed to strengthen family and community life.

Family & Children's Service has been involved in the work of family life education since the 1940s. We offer a range of educational programs designed to help children, youth, and adults build upon their existing assets and to develop new skills and resources to reach their highest potential and to become positive contributors to their communities. These programs are offered in schools, community centers, and other public venues.

Due to the recognized success of these programs and the resulting high demand, Family & Children's Service is now pleased to make our curriculum available to other agencies, community organizations, schools, and businesses that will use the material to help build stronger individuals, families, and communities. For more information, please contact the Family Life Education Department at Family & Children's Service by calling 612-729-0340 or go to our website at www.famchildserv.org.

About Family Life Education

Since 1969, Family & Children's Service, through our Family Life Education (FLE) program has helped people develop life skills and tools for living by providing family life education to clients of diverse ages and cultures. We provide educational and experiential programs for youth in classrooms, small group work with youth and adults in diverse settings, leadership and mentorship opportunities, individual and group work with families in community settings.

In 2000, FLE programs helped more than 4,900 children, youth and adults build upon their existing assets and develop new skills and resources to reach their highest potential and become positive contributors to the community. Time-limited curriculums provide increased knowledge and awareness of issues to foster positive self-images and self-esteem among African-American children and youth, assist youth to successfully cope with a loss in the family due to divorce and death, divert youth from violence and delinquency, deter teenage pregnancy, and provide parents with needed information regarding child-rearing and parenting.

About the Author

Jennifer Simmonds has been with the Family Life Education program of Family & Children's Service since 1999. She has extensive experience in conducting educational and supportive groups with children ages five to 18 throughout Minneapolis on a variety of topics including; grief and loss, coping with significant family change, anger management and conflict resolution, mother-daughter workshops, and issues facing gay, lesbian, and bisexual youth. Ms. Simmonds also frequently conducts individual, specialized presentations on these and other topics for entire classrooms, and school staff. She was previously employed as a Youth Director at a local area church.

Ms. Simmonds has a Masters degree in Education-Youth Development Leadership from the University of Minnesota. She has developed a number of original activities and materials currently used by Family & Children's Service as part of our Family Life Education programs.

Photo by Kathy Kruger.

Family & Children's Service can be contacted at the following address:
414 South Eighth Street
Minneapolis MN
USA 55404-1081

Tel: 612-341-1650
Fax: 612-339-9150
www.famchildserv.org

If you have enjoyed *Seeing Red*,
you may also enjoy related titles from New Society Publishers:

A Volcano in My Tummy
Helping Children to Handle Anger
Éliane Whitehouse and Warwick Pudney

A Volcano in My Tummy presents a clear and effective
approach to helping children and adults alike
understand and deal constructively with children's
anger. The book offers engaging, well-organized
activities which help to overcome the fear of children's
anger which many adult care-givers experience, and
distinguishes between anger the feeling, and violence the
behavior. Primarily created for ages 6 to thirteen, it is
accessible for use in class or at home.

80 pages 8.5" x 11"
40+ line drawings, exercises & games
ISBN 0-86571-349-9
US$12.95 / Can $15.95

Playing with Fire
Creative Conflict Resolution for Young Adults
Fiona Macbeth and Nic Fine

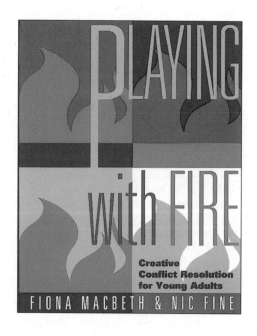

Playing with Fire extends the fast-growing field of conflict
resolution to work with young adults. Drawing from
successful programs in the US, Canada and the UK, it
presents a training program that helps young adults
explore situations of conflict and interpersonal violence
while learning and practicing skills and strategies for
turning destructive conflicts into constructive dialogs. It is
a practical, ready-to-use guide for teachers, counselors,
group leaders, and others.

192 pages 8.5" x 11" Exercises Handouts Reading list
Index
US$19.95 / ISBN 0-86571-306-5
Can$24.95 / ISBN 1-55092-257-2

Free The Children!
Conflict Education for Strong & Peaceful Minds
Susan Gingras Fitzell

Free the Children! offers a unique approach to helping ourselves and our children break free from negative cultural and media conditioning that creates aggression and conflict. Covering pre-K through twelfth grade, it presents five essential components necessary for an effective conflict education curriculum that is developmentally appropriate, and explores key issues including raising a peaceful male child in a violent world; the effect of media violence on children; school bullies; dating violence; and empowering adolescent girls to refuse the role of the "victim."

208 pages 6" x 9"
Resources and handouts
Extensive bibliography
ISBN 0-86571-361-8
US$15.95 / Can$18.95

Keeping the Peace
Practicing Cooperation and Conflict Resolution with Preschoolers
Susanne Wichert

Keeping the Peace is a handbook for parents, daycare providers, kindergarten teachers and playgroup leaders striving to create harmonious groups, bolster children's self-esteem, and foster cooperative and creative interactions between kids aged from two and a half to six. It includes carefully designed and clearly presented activities, anecdotes from the author's own extensive journals, and the theories behind the design.

112 pages 8.5" x 11"
Exercises Photographs Bibliography
US$14.95 / ISBN 0-86571-158-5
Can$17.95 / ISBN 1-55092-031-6

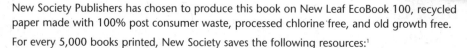